PREACHING WITH POWER
A Sermon Study For Ministers

Study Helps For The Preacher

DR. JOSEPH R. ROGERS, SR.

I. Introduction

The Preaching of The Gospel is a **wonderful, rewarding** and **exciting** ministry. It is a privilege and honor to be called of God to executes such a prestigious **truths** and **insights** to those who are **unsaved, hurting, developing** and **maturing** in the Lord Jesus Christ.

To Preach is **to hurls, throw, teach the word of the Lord** in such a way that, even the babes in Christ will be able to comprehend was is being said.

Throughout the bible there has been many great preachers from all walks of life. This Gospel Message must be preached!

The Apostle Paul summed it up like this, "14 **How then shall they call on him in whom they have not believed? and how shall they believe in him of whom they have not heard? and how shall they hear without a preacher? 15 And how shall they preach, except they be sent? as it is written, How beautiful are the feet of them that preach the gospel of peace and**

bring glad tidings of good things" (Romans 10:15-16)

So, in closing always follow the insights that gave to his son in the ministry, **"Timothy"…**

"I charge thee therefore before God, and the Lord Jesus Christ, who shall judge the quick and the dead at his appearing and his kingdom; [2] Preach the word; be instant in season, out of season; reprove, rebuke, exhort with all longsuffering and doctrine. [3]For the time will come when they will not endure sound doctrine; but after their own lusts shall they heap to themselves teachers, having itching ears; [4] And they shall turn away their ears from the truth, and shall be turned unto fables. [5] But watch thou in all things, endure afflictions, do the work of an evangelist, make full proof of thy ministry.

Be Faithful Unto Death,
Dr. Joseph R. Rogers, Sr.

Table of Contents

II. CHAPTER ONE

(PREACHING, THE PREREQUISITES)

A. THE PREACHER (THE PERSON)

"And that from a child thou hast known the Holy Scriptures, which are able to make thee wise unto salvation through faith which is in Christ Jesus.

All Scripture is given by inspiration of God, and is profitable for doctrine, for reproof, for correction, for instruction in righteousness: That the man of God may be perfect, thoroughly furnished unto all good works". **(II Timothy 3:15-17)**

One who would preach must first, have a personal relationship with the Lord Jesus Christ. He must know from the Scriptures that he has been saved from sin and know what it means to trust Christ alone for salvation. He should be able to teach someone else the basic plan of salvation, that is:

1. God Loves YOU.
   (John 3:16)

2. All have sinned and need salvation.
   (Romans 3:23, Isaiah 64:6)

3. Christ died for our sins.
   (Romans 5:6-9)

4. Christ is the Son of God and God the Son.
   (Matt. 3:17, John 1:1-14)

5. Christ is risen and alive today.
   (I Corinthian 15:3,4)

6. Christ is the only way to Heaven.
   (John 14:6; Acts 4:12)

7. Salvation is a gift, not earned by works.
   (Romans 6:23, Ephesians 2:8,9)

- He/she must maintain a **regular daily devotional life of Bible** reading and prayer. You cannot talk for God if you do not **walk and talk with God.**

- He/she must **believe that the Bible is the Word of God**, and that God has **promised to honor His Word. (Isaiah 55:11)**

- He/she must have a **good testimony** and **a good reputation**, both before the **church** and before the **world. (I Timothy 4:12)**

- His/her own **heart must be right with God**: no sin allowed to remain whether of thought, word or deed. **(Psalm 66:18, I John 1:9)**

- His/her life must be **fully surrendered** to the Lord Jesus Christ. **(Romans 12:1, 2)**

"I'd rather see a sermon than hear one any day; I'd rather one should walk with me than merely tell the way. The eye's a better pupil and more willing than the ear; Fine counsel is confusing, but example's always clear; And the best of all the preachers are the men who live their creeds, for to see good put in action is what everybody needs." **(Edgar Guest)**

III. CHAPTER 2

(THE PROBLEM OF WHAT TO PREACH)

"Woe is unto me, if I preach not the Gospel." **(I Corinthians 9:16)**

"Preach the Word; be instant in season, out of season; reprove, with all longsuffering and doctrine." **(II Timothy 4:2)**

"Go ye into all the world and preach the Gospel to every creature." (St. **Mark 16:15)**

A. It is the message of the Gospel by which we are saved. (I Corinthians 15:1-4).

The essentials of the Gospel are:

- The fact that God is holy, and man is sinful. Christ died and rose again, taking the punishment for our sins.

- Man's best efforts all fall short, and we are hopelessly lost if we trust in our own goodness and efforts.

- God's grace offers a free salvation that cannot in any way be earned or merited.

- We must come to Christ humbly trusting Him alone for our salvation. We must receive it as, a free gift.

- Our assurance of salvation, forgiveness and Heaven are based on the Word of God alone. (**John 5:24, I John 5:13**)

Preaching the Gospel is making the truth of salvation as clear as possible and using enough Scripture so that the Holy Spirit will be able to:

- **Convince from** the truth of the Scriptures

- **Convict of the sin** in the life,

- **Convert the soul** from trusting self to trusting Christ,
- **Change the life** inwardly and outwardly.

Preaching the Gospel is our part. Only the Holy Spirit of God is able to **convince, convict, convert** and **change** lives. The Gospel may be preached with a:

Bible story such as:

- ✓ Naaman II Kings 5:1-14
- ✓ The Brazen Serpent Numbers 21:5-9
- ✓ Nicodemus John 3:1-18
- ✓ The Prodigal Son Luke 15:11-24
- ✓ The Philippian Jailer Acts 16:22-34

Texts such as:

- ✓ Isaiah 45:22---Look and Live! (See Brazen Serpent)
- ✓ Isaiah 53:6---Go in at the first All and come out at the last All.

- ✓ John 1:12---Who are the Children of God?
- ✓ John 3:16-18---The unpardonable sin - terminal unbelief
- ✓ John 3:36---The only two groups of people in the world
- ✓ John 5:24---Passed from death to life!
- ✓ John 6:37---An invitation with a promise!
- ✓ Romans 1:16---God's Dynamite (Gr. Dunamis-power)
- ✓ Romans 4:5,21---God's Grace and our Faith!
- ✓ Romans 5:6-9---Christ died for Ungodly, Us, You.
- ✓ Romans 6:23---God's gift, vs. the devil's wages.
- ✓ Romans 10:9, 10, 13---Believe, Confess openly, Call.

B. <u>It is the preaching and teaching of the Word of God that produces spiritual growth</u>. I Peter 2:2, II Peter 1:2-8

In this process:

a. Be alert to the spiritual needs of the group to which you will be speaking. Are they merely church attenders, or non-attenders? Earnest Christians, or hope-so Christians? Young or old? Those with Bible knowledge, or very little Bible knowledge.

b. Prayerfully search the Scriptures for God's leading as to what you should preach.

c. Take into consideration any special occasion on the calendar, in the news, or in the life of the church. This is often good for the introduction of the message.

d. Keep a notebook or disk file of ideas for sermons. If you get an idea during your daily Bible reading jot it down for later research.

Learn to take notes on sermons you hear or read. (Keep those that are good, get rid of the rest.) Turn to this notebook or file for ideas when you must prepare a message.

e. Remember that in every congregation there may be:

- Sinners who need salvation
- Suffering believers who need comfort
- Backsliders who need restoration
- Carnality that needs to be rebuked
- Errors that need to be corrected
- People who are confused, needing direction

Those who need to be assured that the Lord is real, and that His Word is true.

“THEREFORE, DON'T PREACH YOUR DOUBTS, OR YOUR GRIPES, OR YOUR NOTIONS, YOUR OPINIONS, YOUR POLITICS OR YOUR VIEWS, BUT PREACH THE WORD OF GOD WITH ALL THE AUTHORITY”. THAT GOES WITH IT!

"For we preach not ourselves, but Christ Jesus the Lord; and ourselves your servants for Jesus' sake." **(II Corinthians 4:5)**

IV. CHAPTER THREE

(PREPARATION FOR PREACHING)

"Study to show thyself approved unto God, a workman that needeth not to be ashamed, rightly dividing the Word of truth." **(II Timothy 2:15)**

A. Have an aim or goal. What do you seek to accomplish in the lives of individuals? If you aim at nothing, you will be sure to hit nothing.

You may want to:

- ✓ Win people to Christ
- ✓ Strengthen new Christians
- ✓ Teach some specific doctrine
- ✓ Create a greater love, and worship of the Lord

- ✓ Help in some area of personal living
- ✓ Expose some cult or doctrinal error
- ✓ Challenge believers to live dedicated lives
- ✓ Exhort believers to serve Christ is some specific way

B. You must have a Scriptural foundation for your message

There are three types of sermons:

1. <u>Topical</u> - This method is one theme or topic but using usually us several portions of the Bible to develop the overall teaching of the Bible on the subject. Some good resources materials are:

- The Thompson Chain Reference Bible
- The Nave's Topical Bible

- The New Topical Text Book and others

2. <u>Textual</u> - This method develops an outline from a single verse or a short passage of Scripture.

You will want to check lexicons for meanings of words, and cross references for other verses that will help in the understanding of the passage.
Some helpful materials:

- Online Bible Software with
- Cross-references and lexicons
- The Treasury of Scripture Knowledge
- Vine's Expository of New Testament Words
- Other Reference works and software.

3. <u>Expository</u> - The method involves the teaching of a book or longer passage of the Bible, usually as a series of messages. Consecutive teaching that does not let you ride some hobby or avoid difficult passages. Some helpful materials:

- Bible dictionaries and atlases
- Bible handbooks for background information

C. Do not force the Bible to fit your views. Let the Bible teach you. When the plain sense of Scripture makes common sense, seek no other sense, or you may have nonsense.

D. Every text must be interpreted in the light of its context. **John Wycliffe** wrote, "***It will greatly help thee to understand Scripture if thou mark: (take notice of) not only what is spoke or written, but of whom, and to whom, with what words, at what time, where, to what intent, in what circumstances, considering what goeth before, and what followeth after.***"

E. Be aware of differences. Pay attention to whether God or man or Satan

is speaking. Know the difference between Old & New Testament truth:

O.T. Judaism: Obey and you will be blessed.

N.T. Church: You have all blessings in Christ.

better helpful hints:

- ✓ Is the passage talking to believers or unsaved?
- ✓ Is it a parable (story with a meaning) or an event?
- ✓ Is it appropriate for today?

F. Keep in mind some definitions of terms:

a. Inspiration refers to God's stamp of accuracy and authority on that which is recorded in the Bible.

b. Revelation refers to those parts of the Bible revealed by God that would not otherwise be known.

(Illustration: Historical sections of the Bible are inspired, but not a revelation of otherwise unknown information.)

c. **Illumination** is when the Holy Spirit makes a Bible truth clear as a believer reads the Bible.

d. **Interpretation** is determining what the passage meant when it was written.

e. **Application** is the way we use a portion of Scripture to meet a present need.

There is only one correct interpretation to any portion of the Bible, but there may be many applications.

G. Make notes! Lots of notes! (If you are doing it on computer, print it out, sort it out, and then put it in order on your word processor.)

If you are doing it on paper, keep all notes on one side. (Many good ideas get lost because they were on the back of a sheet of paper.)

Collect your ideas, key verses, quotations, poems, illustrations, etc. Spread them out, pray about it, and put them in order.

DWIGHT L. MOODY ON SERMON PREPARATION

"I have no secret. I study more by subjects than I do by texts. If when I am reading, I meet a good thing on any of these subjects, I slip it into the right envelope and leave it there.

I always carry a notebook, and if I hear anything in a sermon that will throw light on that subject, I put it down and slip it into the envelope.

Perhaps I let it lie for a year or more. When I want a new sermon, I take everything that has been accumulating. Between what I find there and the results of my own study I have material enough.

I am all the time going over my sermons, taking out a little here and adding a little there. In that way they never get very old. I am never ashamed to repeat a sermon."

(D.L. MOODY LIVED BEFORE THE TIME OF FILE FOLDERS, SO HE USED LARGE ENVELOPES WITH TOPIC NAMES ON THEM. IN THIS DAY OF COMPUTERS, IT IS MUCH EASIER TO COMPILE INFORMATION.)

DEVELOP YOUR MESSAGE TOWARD A CLIMAX, NOT JUST A CONCLUSION. KEEP YOUR GOAL OR AIM IN MIND.

A message is not just 3 points and a poem. It is not just a way to fill up 30 minutes of time.

People have come for a message from God for their souls. We dare not give them anything less

There was an old uneducated preacher from the south who was asked how he prepared his sermons.

His answer was, "I read myself full, think myself clear, pray myself hot, and then I let's go!" Perhaps he had something.

V. CHAPTER 4

(THE PATTERN FOR THE SERMON)

"For after that in the wisdom of God the world by wisdom knew not God, it pleased God by the foolishness of preaching to save them that believe." (I Corinthians 1:21)

"Let all things be done decently and in order." (I Corinthians 14:40)

A. <u>A sermon must have an introduction</u>.

Often the introduction will make the difference in whether the congregation will pay attention to the sermon.

a. The purposes of the introduction:

- To get the attention of the people

- To arouse interest in the subject

- To introduce your text or topic

- To relate the subject to some occasion

- To make the people want to listen

b. The introduction may be:

- ✓ A rhetorical question - one you will answer
- ✓ Your text
- ✓ An observation or illustration
- ✓ A quotation on your subject. (You may agree or
- ✓ disagree with the person quoted.)
- ✓ The background of your Scripture passage

B. <u>A sermon needs a well-organized body of truth so that God's people will not go away hungry and the unsaved will not go away unaware of their need of Christ as Savior</u>.

The body of the message may have several points, but only one aim or purpose. The truths presented should be illustrated out of present day living, and then applied to current experience. Always…

- **State the truth**
- **Illustrate the truth**
- **Apply the truth**

C. A sermon should have a CLIMAX, NOT JUST A CONCLUSION. The entire sermon should build toward this to accomplish the aim of the sermon.

I heard a preacher deliver an excellent message, with a heart-touching illustration of leading a person to Christ on their death-bed.

The aim was accomplished, but the preacher had more in his outline, and he went on to finish the outline.

He could have given an invitation at the end of the illustration and forgotten the rest of his outline and he would have been far more effective.

YOU DO NOT HAVE TO TEACH EVERYTHING YOU KNOW OR HAVE salesman - close when you have made the sale.

A conclusion may be a poem, an effective illustration, or some other portion of Scripture that reinforces your text.

D. The conclusion of a sermon may tie the whole sermon together, and end with an invitation or a challenge. A SERMON SHOULD HAVE ONLY ONE CONCLUSION!

E. A sermon is a message from God's Word that should inform the mind, stir the emotions, and move the will to action or a decision.

F. The preacher should double check the sermon for aim, clarity, doctrinal accuracy, good illustrations, and a message from God, not just the preacher.

NEVER ASSUME THAT EVERYONE IN FRONT OF YOU IS REALLY SAVED. ALWAYS INCLUDE THE GOSPEL IN SOME WAY.

G. "Sir, we would see Jesus." (John 12:21)

VI. CHAPTER FIVE

(THE PRESENTATION OF THE SERMON)

Public speaking takes various forms.

A lecturer presents a set of opinions, views or truths for the information of the hearers.

A political speaker presents his or her position on issues with a view to persuading the audience to agree or support that position.

A teacher presents information in a way that he or she may analyze how much has been learned. This is done by examination, discussion or other participation.

A sermon is the presentation of Biblical truth in a way that will warm the heart, challenge the mind, and affect the life. It may lead to an invitation to respond for salvation, dedication or other commitment.

A model for preaching is in Nehemiah 8:8.

"So, the read in the book of the law distinctly, and gave the sense, and caused them to understand the reading." Nehemiah 8:8

A. **Preaching is communicating God's truth**. Learn how to project your voice so that even without a public-address system you will be heard clearly in the back row.

Don't shout but speak from the diaphragm. Don't use a "Holy tone." or "preacher voice." Speak a little more slowly than you normally do.

****Stand up to be seen**

****Speak up to be heard**

****Sit down to be appreciated**

(Some of us learned this as Stand up, speak up and shut up. Some never learned the last point.)

B. The text of Nehemiah 8:8 gives an outline of the simplest and best kind of preaching.

- Distinct Bible reading - State Clearly.
- Gave the sense - explained and illustrated.
- Caused them to understand - present application.

C. The apostle Paul had a burdened heart "I am debtor." (Romans 1:14)

The preacher must have a love for the Lord and a concern for souls. Be earnest. Put your heart into your preaching.

D. Paul also had a prepared mind.

"I am ready" (Romans 1:15)

Being well prepared is essential to a good message. Being well prepared is the best way to overcome fear or stage fright. Remember, people have come for a message from God for their souls. Dare we give them less than our best?

E. We have a glorious Gospel!

"I am not ashamed." (Romans 1:16)

Have a vision of the holiness of God, the sinfulness of sin, the lostness of the lost, the reality of Heaven and Hell, and PREACH FOR A VERDICT!

F. Ask God's blessing on His Word before and after the sermon.

G. Keep records!

Your memory is not perfect. Keep a final outline as a record of what you preached. Make notations on the back of it as to date, place, results, etc. You may want to keep a paper or computer file (database) of such things as: Subject, Text, Title, date, place, and possibly a consecutive number.

"I love to tell the story, 'tis pleasant to repeat What seems each time I tell it, More wonderfully sweet. I love to tell the story, For some have never heard The message of salvation From God's own Holy Word. I love to tell the story, 'Twill be my theme in glory To tell the old, old story of Jesus and His love".

SOME GOSPEL OUTLINES FOR PREACHING:

(God must do the saving. Merely using a formula or an outline does not guarantee results. Pray for God's blessing on His Word. He has promised that it will not return to Him void.))

****THE ROMAN ROAD TO SALVATION**

WHO IS GOOD ENOUGH FOR GOD'S HEAVEN? NO ONE. As it is written, there is none righteous, no, not one: **(Romans 3:10)**

****WHO HAS SINNED? EVERYONE**. or all have sinned, and come short of the glory of God; **(Romans 3:23)**

****HOW CAN I EARN SALVATION**? YOU CAN'T. But to him that

worketh not, but believeth on him that justifieth the ungodly, his faith is counted for righteousness. **(Romans 4:5)**

****HOW CAN ANYONE BE SAVED**? TRUST CHRIST ALONE. For when we were yet without strength, in due time Christ died for the ungodly. For scarcely for a righteous man will one die: yet peradventure for a good man some would even dare to die. But God commendeth his love toward us, in that, while we were yet sinners, Christ died for us. **(Romans 5:6-8)**

****SALVATION MUST BE RECEIVED AS A FREE GIFT**. For the wages of sin is death; but the gift of God is eternal life through Jesus Christ our Lord. **(Romans 6:23)**

****CAN I BE SURE I AM SAVED**? YES! There is therefore now no condemnation to them which are in Christ Jesus, who walk not after the flesh, but after the Spirit. **(Romans 8:1)**

**WHAT SHOULD I DO? BELIEVE IN CHRIST AND CONFESS HIM OPENLY BEFORE MEN. ACKNOWLEDGE HIM AS YOUR SAVIOUR.

"That if thou shalt confess with thy mouth the Lord Jesus, and shalt believe in thine heart that God hath raised him from the dead, thou shalt be saved. For with the heart man believeth unto righteousness; and with the mouth confession is made unto salvation". (Romans 10:9,10)

GOD'S PROMISE.

"For whosoever shall call upon the name of the Lord shall be saved". (Romans 10:13)

<u>**"THE GOSPEL ON YOUR FINGERS"**</u>

****I HAVE SINNED:**

(Thumb points toward me)

"For all have sinned and come short of the glory of God". **(Romans 3:23)**

**GOD LOVES ME:
(First finger points to Heaven)

"For God so loved the world, that he gave his only begotten Son, that whosoever believeth in him should not perish, but have everlasting life". (John 3:16)

**CHRIST DIED FOR ME:
(Middle finger longest, important)

"For I delivered unto you first that which I Also received, how that Christ died for our sins according to the scriptures". (1 Corinthians 15:3)

**I RECEIVE HIM AS MY PERSONAL SAVIOUR: (Ring finger)

"But as many as received him, to them gave he power to become the sons of God, even to them that believe on his name: (John 1:12)

**I AM SAVED:
(Little finger)

“And they said, believe on the Lord Jesus Christ, and Thou shalt be saved, and thy house. (Acts 16:31)

THE A - B - C OF SALVATION

A - Admit that you are a sinner in God's sight.

B - Believe that Christ died for you.

C - Come to Him, Call on Him, Confess Him openly before men.

The "ALL" Plan of Salvation

“For all have sinned and come short of the glory of God”. **(Romans 3:23)**

But we are all as an unclean thing, and **all our righteousness** are as filthy rags; and we all do fade as a leaf; and our iniquities, like the wind, have taken us away. **(Isaiah 64:6)**

“All we like sheep have gone astray; we have turned everyone to his own way; and the LORD hath laid on him the iniquity of us all”. **(Isaiah 53:6)**

FOUR THINGS GOD DOES NOT KNOW

God does not know of any sin that He does not hate.

God does not know of any sinner He does not love.

God does not know of any other way of salvation than the cross of Christ.

God does not know any better time to trust Christ than RIGHT NOW.

(Some Fully Text Sermons)

"The God Of A Second Chance"
A Sermon By Dr. Joseph R. Rogers, Sr.
For The Mount Zion First Baptist Church
Rocky Mount, North Carolina 27804
Theme: The Power of "Grace' & "Mercy"
July 9, 2017

Scripture: "And the word of the Lord came unto **Jonah** the **'second time'**. Saying, Arise, go unto **Nin-e-vet**, that great city, and **'preach'** unto it the **preaching** that **I bid (told you) thee". (Jonah 3:1,2)**

Introduction

My brothers and sisters, I'm glad God **gives second chances**! I have made **plenty of mistakes** in my life. I'm **certainly glad** God didn't **"give up"** on me **like others**, but instead He keeps **stretching forth** His hands of **'grace'** and **'mercy'**.

One of the great lessons of Jonah's **'failure'** and **'forgiveness'** is that God will still use those who return to Him; not that God, **condones** (approves) their short-comings, but **'forgives'** and **'restored'** them; thereafter, and use them in a mighty way.

Just like Jonah, many **spiritual leaders** received a **'second chance'** to do what God called him to do.

- ✓ **Adam** sinned in the garden and God covered him.
- ✓ **Moses** murdered a man and God called and anointed him.
- ✓ **Elijah** complained and quit, and God re-commissioned him.
- ✓ **Peter** denied the Lord and then God used him at Pentecost.
- ✓ **John Mark** deserted the mission trip; yet God anointed him to write the second Gospel.

It is a fact, beloved; **"If It had not been for the Lord on their and our sides,** the question is, **"Where would we be"?** Well, I believe that we already know the answer: We would be **doomed** and **destroyed**!

I want all who are under the sound of my voice to know that, I am not **advocating, willfully sinning**, but we must never forget that, absent the power of God we are **“helpless”.**

Yes! There is an old church hymn that sheds some light on the issue that give use the joy and assurance of knowing that God cares…: Listen at the lyrics…

(Verse One)

“Without Him (Jesus) we would be nothing, Without Him (Jesus), we would fail, Without Him (Jesus), we would be drifting, like a ship without a sail.”

(Verse Two)

“Without Him (Jesus) I could be dying, Without Him (Jesus) I'd be enslaved, Without Him (Jesus) life would be hopeless, But with Jesus, Thank God, I'm saved”

Human nature (The Flesh) tends to have a quick answer or solution to others **‘shortcomings’**–God do them in; but will, contrastly, apply elastic to their own faults—God have mercy!

I believe that he **Body of Christ** would be **healthier,** if we learn how to—**build each other up, rather than tear each other down!**

I believe the **body of Christ would be healthier**, if we learn the art of **encouraging each other, rather than put each other down!**

I believe the **body of Christ would be healthier**, if we learn the art of having each other back, rather than digging ditches of destruction.

Getting a **'second chance'** is not based upon trying to **get over of the Lord**, but **'truly repenting'** of ones' **'sins and short-comings'**. I would not **advise** anyone to try to **do a number on God**. Anyone who tries to **out maneuver God**, we all get the short end of the stick…and will find **themselves wanting**!!ask…

- **The Prophets of Baal** as they Challenged The Prophet Elijah on Mount Carmel
- **Jezebel** as she put out a death warrant out on The Prophet Elijah for telling the truth.
- **Belshazzar** has he defied the vessels in the Holy Temple and threw a party desecrating them.

My brothers and sisters, I thank the Lord that He has **stretched forth** His hands of ***"mercy" and "grace"*** to mankind. Without **"Grace"** and **"Mercy"** we would be **eternally separated** from the Lord:

Exposition I

In the text, **Jonah too received a "second chance"**. And you and I many times, **after salvation**, like **Jonah**, we find ourselves in **need of a 'second chance'**. You know the times **I'm talking about**? It is no one here that have crossed every **"T"** and dotted ever **"I"**. **The times when…**

- ✓ We made **a "total disaster" of our lives**.

- ✓ We **"turned a deaf ear" to God principles and plan.**
- ✓ We **"felt as though"** we could walk this journey without God.

In our experiences and specifically, in Jonah's God used **"a mighty storm"**, and **"three days" and "nights"** in the belly of **a fish** to get **Jonah's attention**.

The story of Jonah isn't about a **"fish"**. It's about the God of the **"second chance"**. Jonah, a prophet, had been commanded by God to preach to the **citizens of Nineveh** the capital of the **nation of Assyria**.

Telling Jonah that he was to preach and minister to the **'Assyrians'** was like asking:

- A **'Jew'** the shake the hand of a Samaritan,
- A **'KKK'** to back in the day to shake the hand of a black man,
- A **'Native Indian'** to shake the hand of Old Pale Face,

Nothing would have pleased The Prophet Jonah more than to see the whole bunch of the **Assyrians wiped off the earth**. Those Assyrians may have mattered to God, but they didn't matter to Jonah.

God told Jonah to travel **'east'** over land to **Nineveh**, but he booked passage on a ship headed **'west'** toward **Spain.** During that journey, a tremendous **storm arose,** and Jonah ended up in the **Mediterranean Sea**.

Within a short time of gulping down the Prophet, the fish suffered an attack of **indigestion**. When we do not **follow God's Plan** for our lives it will affect those around us.

In this text, God allowed Jonah to **survive** being swallowed by that fish: inside of the **fish intestines**; symbolic of HELL! Thanks be to God would give us **'second chances'**.

You might have thought that God would have **given up on Jonah** and **drafted** another prophet easier to work with. But,

I am here to tell all of us that, “**What God has for you and for your to do, is for you**”!

But, in the middle of the book of Jonah there is an interesting phrase. **Jonah 3:1** says, **“Then word of the Lord came to Jonah a second time.”** Now, deliberately, consciously, stubbornly, Jonah had run away from God.

Yet, God came to the prophet a **second time** and allowed him to carry on his ministry. That's an important lesson from the story of Jonah...”**God is the God of the second chance**”.

So, what is it that we can “**learn**” from Jonah’s second chance experience? How can we and “**apply**” these principles to our lives and How can we take the message and “**help**” others.

I. We Need A Second Chance “When…”: (1:2-3)

We evade (shirk, dodge) our responsibilities. The Lord instructed Jonah to go the ‘**Nineveh**’ and “**CRY**” against it. But, Jonah arose and went the opposite—to **Tarshish** from the **presence of the Lord**.

You see, Jonah was not **guilty** of **'knowing what to do'**, but **'refusing to do it.** Yes! Jonah wanted to get as **far away** as he could from his **responsibilities as possible**. I must tell us that…

A. FAILURE IS NOT FINAL (vs. 1).

The nation of Israel sinned, but God give her a **'second chance'**. Neither do our **failures need to be final**. The **true character** of a person is seen in how **'defeats'**, **'set-backs'** and **'challenges'** are handled.

You may feel **'defeated'** today. You might feel as though you are not qualified for the job. You might feel as those God should **'send or use'** someone else.

Just remember, many of God's people have had to **'overcome' defeats, image problems**, and **doubts** to gain victory.

a. Abraham (lying), b. Samson (women), c. Peter (arrogance)

d. John Mark (quitting), e. David (Bathsheba) and f. Elijah (self-pity)

And today, my friends, God will give you and me a **second chance;** only if we do as stated in **1 John 1:9'**-"[9] **If we confess our sins, he is faithful and just to forgive us our sins, and to cleanse us from all unrighteousness." God will give is VICTORY…**

- **a. over alcohol,**
- **b. over sexual sins**
- **c. over poor examples,**
- **d. over divorce**
- **e. over greed,**
- **f. over gossip**
- **g. over selfishness,**
- **h. over poor decision**

Well, my brothers and my sister **evading** ones' responsibilities, **robs us of God's manifold blessings**. The "**irony**" of this story is: **Running from** God exhausted Jonah, so much so, that he **"slept" during a fierce storm.**

The Apostle Paul's admonishes us about **sleeping** saying…

1 Thessalonians 5:6-"THEREFORE LET US NOT SLEEP, AS DO OTHERS; BUT LET US WATCH AND BE SOBER."

The Disciple Peter's **heavy eyelids** caused him to **deny the Lord.**

St. Luke 22:46-"AND SAID UNTO THEM, WHY SLEEP YE? RISE AND PRAY, LEST YE ENTER INTO TEMPTATION."

But, my brothers and my sister Our **enemy (Satan)** never sleeps.

St. Matthew 13:25-"BUT WHILE MEN "SLEPT", HIS ENEMY CAME AND "SOWED TARES" AMONG THE "WHEAT", AND WENT HIS WAY."

Exposition II

II. We Get A Second Chance When: (1:11-12)

We realize we have blown it and admit that fact. Jonah said take me and **'cast'** me off into the sea, to that all we be calm. **Jonah knew what the deal was- he knew the anointing that we on his**

life. It is a fact we can run, but we cannot hide!

King David also is another one who blew it but got a **second chance.**

Psalm 32:5-"I ACKNOWLEDGED MY SIN UNTO THEE, AND MINE INIQUITY HAVE I NOT HID. I SAID, I WILL CONFESS MY TRANSGRESSIONS UNTO THE LORD; AND THOU FORGAVEST THE INIQUITY OF MY SIN. SELAH."

My brothers and sisters we must admit that Jonah is **not alone in the fine art of blowing it**, he has **plenty of company!** Particularly, You and me! But, the Lord is good! All we should do is like Jonah…

Jonah 'prayed'–God heard his 'prayers'!!
Jonah 'remembered' that God is 'deliverer'!!

Conclusion

So, as I close this message, I am glad to **know that,**

- **The God of Israel,**
- **The God of Stilling The Storms,**
- **The God of Turing our sadness in to Joy,**
- **The God Who is Able and Willing,**
- **The God of a second chance!**

He is so merciful! Why? Because he **knows and cares about us**!

- ✓ He knows how to **'fix'** what has been **broken,**
- ✓ **He knows how mend what has been torn,**
- ✓ **He knows how to build up what has been destroyed** and it does not matter how:

Far **'down' you are--God can **pick you up.**

Far **‘up’ you are-God can **bring you down**.

- I am talking about **The God of Compassion!**
- I am talking about **The God of Love!**
- I am talking about **The God Of A Second Chance!**

What happens when we get that **second chance**? People around and attached to us will receive the **needed ‘good news’ (Jonah 2:4-7)** and **“our burdens” will be lifted, and sins forgiven**.

King David puts it this way, **Psalm 51:12-"RESTORE UNTO ME THE ‘JOY’ OF THY SALVATION; AND UPHOLD ME WITH THY FREE SPIRIT..."**

I Thank God today for The God of a **“SECOND CHANCE”**! God is **calling us** to be **“Messengers Bearers” giving out His Word** to the world.

- Are you tired of **the self-induced storms**?
- Are you tired of **going east, when you should be going west**?
- Are you tired of **holding the Word of God inside of you?**
- Are you tried of **being thrown overboard into the seas of life?**
- Are you tired of **experiencing sea weed and water of life?**
- Are you tired of **being swallowed up by** the **whales of life?**
- Are you tired of **the uncomfortable belly of the whales of life**?
- Are you tired of **giving the people ingestion, heartburn**?
- Are you tired of **making people sick of the stomach?**

Well, I have some good news! Cry out to the God of a **"Second Chance"**, remembering the saying of Charles Wesley, verses one and two:

"Father, I stretch my hands to Thee,
No other help I know;

If Thou withdraw Thyself from me,
Ah! whither shall I go?

What did Thine only Son endure,
Before I drew my breath!

What pain, what labor, to secure, My soul from endless death!"

I am a living witness without **reservation, hesitation**--He will! He will! He will do it! Why? Because…

I. God Is Merciful:

Psalms 100:5-"For the LORD is good; his mercy is everlasting; and his truth endureth to all generations".

II. God Is Patient:

Romans 15:5,6-"[5] Now the God of patience and consolation grant you to be likeminded one toward another according to Christ Jesus: [6] That ye may with one mind and one mouth glorify God, even the Father of our Lord Jesus Christ".

III. God Is Long-suffering:

Numbers 14:18-"The LORD is longsuffering, and of great mercy, forgiving iniquity and transgression".

IV. God Is Just:

1 John 1:9,10-"If we confess our sins, he is faithful and just to forgive us our sins, and to cleanse us from all unrighteousness. 10If we say that we have not sinned, we make him a liar, and his word is not in us".

"And the word of the Lord came unto **Jonah** the **'second time'**. Saying, Arise, go unto **Nin-e-veh**, that great city, and **'preach'** unto it the **preaching** that **I bid (told you) thee"**. **(Jonah 3:1,2)**

"The God Of A Second Chance"

Joseph R. Rogers, Sr., D. Min., Servant
Mount Zion First Baptist Church
Rocky Mount, North Carolina 27804

"The Cohesiveness Of The Church"

A Sermon By Dr. Joseph R. Rogers, Sr.
For St. James Missionary Baptist Church
Rocky Mount, North Carolina 27801
Theme: The Glue of The Body of Christ
June 25, 2017

Scripture: "And I say also unto thee, that thou art **Peter**, and upon this" Rock" I will **build My Church**; and the **"Gates Of Hell"** shall not **prevail against it..."** **(St. Matthew 16:18, 19)**

Cohesive: sturdy; the ability to bond or holding together; glue.

Introduction

As we come today in celebration of **"Homecoming"**, it is indeed a privilege and honor to be in the house of the Lord. We know that if it had not been for The Lord, our being here would not be possible.

Whether we realize it not, really church in the center and core of who we are, and we will ever become. The bible is right and will always be right, "It is

God who **gifts us, talent us, enable us, guide us, sustains us, justifies us, equips us and the same who will one day "glorify"** us!

- While we are here, let us lift Him up, **higher and higher**: that is, He who is able to do exceedingly, abundantly above all that you and I could ever think or ask!

- While we are here, let us lift Him up, **higher and higher**: that is, He who while we were yet sinners died for us!

- While we are here, let us lift Him up **higher and higher**: that is, He who will hid us in the pavilion!

Yes! It is the church and a relationship with Jesus that has gotten all of us over the **"HUMP".**

Yes! It is the church who have pick us up, turned us around and place our feet on solid ground.

Yes! It is the church that has been our bridge of troubled waters and rock in a weary land!

Much has been said over the years concerning the **'cohesiveness'** the Church of Our Lord Jesus Christ. Some say that The Church is" losing" **Her spiritual effectiveness, "losing", Her ability to influence the secular world, "losing", Her ability to Light the darkness of the world,** and **"losing", Her ability to exhibit a seasoning flavor upon the earth.**

I beg the difference, Because, I trust God and His word, I rebut and challenge such **accusations**. Why? Because, the church has **"now"**, the same power She has always had since Her conception—She possesses **"Power" over all principalities and powers of evil".**

Just, because there are a **few problems** that seems to persist; a few persons that **bring reproach** on the church; a **few people walking away** in difficult times; by no means **prove** or

suggest that the **"Most Powerful Institution"** on the face of the earth, is ***losing or have lost its authority or influence.***

- ✓ The Church, **Our House of Refuge,**
- ✓ The Church, **Our Solid Foundation,**
- ✓ The Church, **Our House of Prayer,**
- ✓ The Church **Our Place of Deliverance,**

✓ The Church **Our Pavilion of Praise and Worship**…is in no way falling way, losing Her authority, effectiveness or efficiency or guiding light!

The Church has been the **"guiding light"** of the world for many years and has **help many people** *turn* their lives around from the dark pit of darkness into the **marvelous light of Jesus Christ**!

The church has and will always play an **integral role** in transforming the lives of mankind. She has changed…

- **Pips into Preacher!**
- **Ladies of the night into Saint of the light!**
- **Liars into men/women of Greater Character and Integrity!**
- **Sinners into Saints!**
- **Doubter into Believers!**

It is without question, my brothers and sister that we are assured that **"The Church of The Living God"** will **"LIVE"**, **"WELL"** and will **"PREVAIL"** forever. Why? Because, She is endowed with **power** and **authority** that will never be conquered, by any force!

"The Cohesiveness of The Church"

Exposition I

The Church has been challenged for many centuries, by many generations, and on many occasions; yet to no avail:

- **Nations** have tried to discredit her name;
- **Kings & Queens** have tired overthrown her rule;

- **Armies of Great Militaries** have tried to defeat her; and
- **Individuals** have tried to overtake, but all to no avail.
- ***Perverted Religious Groups* have tried to become her.**
- **The Traditions of Men** have taken a **"punch"** at her

But we are assured that **"The Church of Our Lord"** will prevail forever. Jesus Christ said very confidently, ***"Heaven and Earth would pass away, before one jot or till of My Word fail".***

So, why has **no other force** in the earth been able to **"conquer"** the Spirit of The Living God? God is **invincible, unconquerable** and no one will be able to **weaken or overthrow**--The King of kings & Lord of lords.

The attacks on the Church of God keep coming daily, but the more they come the **stronger** the members of the body of Christ become. We're built on a **solid foundation** that has and will continue to withstand **the strong winds of challenges** and **the violet waves of life**—we will stand!

"The Cohesiveness of The Church"

Exposition II

Our text shows us why the **"Church"**—the universal organism is alive and well today. Let us now examine some of the reason the church is **prevailing even** in this age The New Age Movement:

I. The Foundation Is Right: (Jesus Christ) (St. Matt. 16:18)

St. Matthew 16:18-"[18] And I say also unto thee, That thou art Peter, and upon this rock I will build my church; and the gates of hell shall not prevail against it".

1 Corinthian 3:11-"[11] For other foundation can no man lay than that is laid, which is Jesus Christ".

In the first scripture, Jesus said "Upon this **"rock" (Peter =petro, petra)**, I will build **my church**". There is not another like this foundation. This foundation is **solid, sure, steadfast** and **unmovable**.

In the second scripture, The Apostle Paul said, ***"For other foundations can no man lay than that is laid, which is Jesus Christ"***. *JESUS* is the **"brain"** and the **"heart"** beat of the ***total operation***, (The Body–Church) and He is like a tree that's planted by the water of the river that shall never be moved or removed.

I am so glad today to know that," My **hope is built on nothing less, than Jesus Blood and Righteousness, because I dare not trust the sweetest frame, but Holy, Holy lean on Jesus Name: On Christ the solid "Rock" I stand all, all, all other ground is sinking sand".**

Don't build your house on a" foundation" that has **"sand"** beneath its structure, because if you do, when the **strong winds blow,** and the **trials of this life comes**, you will have no sure anchor to hold on too.

My Beloved, I am happy to announce that, **our anchor** is "**sure**", very sure and it will hold—come hell or high water, because we are attached to "The Solid Rock", Jesus Christ.

In Jesus Christ, **"The Church"** have standing power: The Apostle Paul told the church at Corinth in, **II Corinthians 4:7-12-"[7] But we have this treasure in earthen vessels, that the excellency of the power may be of God, and not of us. [8] *We are* troubled on every side, yet not distressed; *we are* perplexed, but not in despair; [9] Persecuted, but not forsaken; cast down, but not destroyed".**

"The Cohesiveness of The Church"

II. *The Leadership Is Right:* (Good Leaders) (Ephesians 4:11-13; 5:23)

Ephesian 4:11-13-"And He gave some Apostles; and some Prophets; and some Evangelist, and some Pastors and Teachers; for the edifying of the body of Christ: Till we all come in the unity of the faith, and of the knowledge of The Son of God, unto a perfect man, unto the

measure of the stature of the fullness of Christ" (Ephesians 4:11-13),

Ephesian 5:23a-" 23b …, even as Christ is the head of the church: and He is the Savior of the body.

1 Timothy 2:5- "5 For *there is* one God, and one mediator between God and men, the man Christ Jesus".

If any organization is going to **move ahead** and become **fruitful** there must be at the Top, **Good Leadership**. The Lord Jesus Christ is the Head of The Church– and our Great High Priest!

- ✓ **He is King of kings and Lord of lords…**
- ✓ **The Stem of Jesse,**
- ✓ **The Rod of David…**
- ✓ **The Tribe of Judah…**
- ✓ **The Rock upon a Rock.**

And all **"Power"** has been given unto Him in Heaven and Earth…of which He has a Name that is above all others names---**at this name every knee should bow, every**

tongue should confess—that He (Jesus) Is Lord. Jesus Christ **established** His Church and **called, commissioned** and **anointed** Leadership to carry out His Plan and Mission. **Next…**

"The Cohesiveness of The Church"

III. *The Commission Is Right*: (The Charge) (St. Matthew 28:18-20; St. Mark 16:15, 16)

As with any organization, **Plans** must be made for its mission and vison. There need to be **a clear sense of directions**—that is, we are to write the vision and make it plain. Remember, we can't go anywhere if we don't have some sense of direction.

St. Matthew 28:18-20-" [18] And Jesus came and spake unto them, saying, **All power** is given unto me in heaven and in earth.[19] Go ye therefore, and **teach all nations, baptizing them in the name of the Father, and of the Son, and of the Holy Ghost**: [20] **Teaching them** to observe all things whatsoever I have commanded you: and, **lo, I am with you always, even**

unto the end of the world. Amen". (St. Matthew 28:19-20)

St. Mark 16:15, 16-"And He said unto them, Go ye into all the world, and Preach the Gospel to Every Creature. He that believeth and is baptized shall be "saved"; but he that believeth not shall be damned".

It is without question that the **"Commission"**–The Command, The Directives, Instructions, Charge, and Assignment to the Church is right. Let us **move forward** doing the **'Master's Will'** and complete the assignment that has been given to us. **Next…**

IV. ***The Doctrine Is Right*****: (Rules & Regulations) (1 Timothy 3:15; Jude 1:3)**

1 Timothy 3:15-"[15] But if I tarry long, that *thou mayest know how* thou oughtest to behave thyself in the *House Of The Lord*, which *is the church* of The Living God, the Pillar and Ground of the Truth".

Jude 1:3-"[3b] …, and exhort you that ye should earnestly contend for the faith which was once delivered unto the saints.

My brothers and sisters, any organization must have ***"rules"*** and ***"regulations"***, if it is to be correctly guided, because where there are **no guidelines**, things will become **chaotic.**

The Great King Solomon said, **"Let us hear the conclusion (the end of the matter) of the whole matter: *Fear God* and *keep His commandments*: for this is the" whole duty" of man". (Eccl. 12:13)**

The Lord Jesus Christ makes it clear to us that He said, "I am the Way, the Truth, and the Life: and *no man* cometh to the Father, but by Me." **Next…**

"The Cohesiveness of The Church"

V. *The Rewards Are Right*: (Benefits) (Revelations 22:12)

Revelations 22:12- "[12] And, Behold I come quickly; and my *"reward"* is with Me, to give every man according as his work shall be".

My brothers and sisters, all that you and I will have ever, or will ever **contended** here on this earth will be **worth it all of the pain, agony and frustration.**

We will be **tried, tested** and **tempted**, but through it all, but rest assured, we will arise as **"More Than Conquerors"**, **"Victors and not Victims"**, **"Above and not Beneath"** and **"The Head and not The Tail"** through Jesus Christ.

If we can but **hold on and hold out**– this to will pass! We will **shout, praise** and **dance** the victory as:

- ✓ **Israel** did after crossing the Red Sea and Jordan River!
- ✓ **David** did after defeating The Giant Goliath!
- ✓ **Elijah** did after overthrowing the prophets of Baal!
- ✓ **Paul & Silas** after singing and praying in jail!

1 Corinthians 2:9-"[9] But it is written, Eyes have not seen, nor ears

heard, neither has it entered into the *"hearts of Men"*, the things that God has prepared for them that *Love Him*".

2 Timothy 4:8-"[8] Henceforth there is laid up for me a *crown of righteousness*, which the Lord, the *righteous Judge*, shall give me at that day: and not to me only, but unto *all them* also that *Love* his appearing".

Conclusion

So, in conclusion, I would hope that you have a better picture concerning the **"Cohesiveness"** (Bonding) of the Church. This Organism **is not going anywhere, it is not falling down**, but most of all **it will never be conquered.**

- ✓ Jesus Christ is our ***Foundation***: Our Anchor!
- ✓ Jesus Christ is our ***Leader***: The Good Shepherd!
- ✓ Jesus Christ is our ***Doctrine***: The Word- (Rules & Regulations)
- ✓ Jesus Christ is our ***Guide***: The Head of the Church

That is why we can sing with JOY, as the Songwriter has said," On **Christ the**

solid rock I stand, all other ground is sinking sand, I dare not trust the sweetest frame, but holy, holy, lean on Jesus' name...etc." **We *Must Stand On* the Promises of Christ Our Savior!**

Another Songwriter has said, **"Standing on the promises of Christ my King, Through eternal ages let His praises ring, Glory in the highest, I will shout and sing, Standing on the promises of God.**

(Refrain)

Standing, standing, Standing, on the promises of God my Savior; Standing, standing, I'm standing on the promises of God.

"<u>The Cohesiveness of The Church</u>"

Joseph R. Rogers, Sr., D. Min., Pastor
Mt. Zion 1st Baptist Church
Rocky Mount, NC

VII. The Author's Contact Information and Other Works

A. Email Address:

jroger3420@aol.com,

HOW TO WALK
IN YOUR DESTINY
"YOUR PATHWAY
TO VICTORY"
DR. JOSEPH R.
ROGERS, SR.

MY ROLE IN
THE LOCAL
CHURCH
STAY IN
YOUR LANE
UNITY
DR. JOSEPH ROOSEVELT
ROGERS SR.

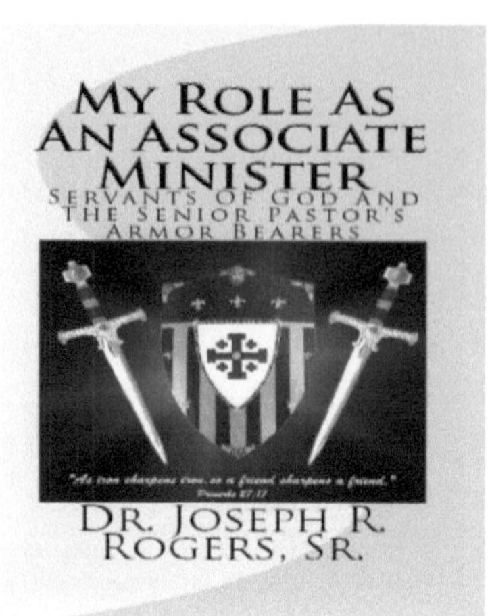
My Role As
An Associate
Minister
Servants Of God And
The Senior Pastor's
Armor Bearers
Dr. Joseph R.
Rogers, Sr.

Christian
Discipleship And
The Holy Spirit
Equipping For
And Engaging In
Christian Warfare
Dr. Joseph Roosevelt
Rogers Sr.

MARRIAGE
GOD'S WAY
"KEEP THE FIRE
BURNING"
DR. JOSEPH R. ROGERS, SR.

CHURCH
LEADERSHIP
THE PASTOR AND
THE DEACON
GOD
DR. JOSEPH R. ROGERS SR.

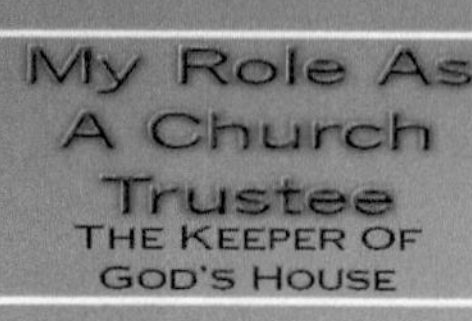

EVANGELISM
101
"TEARING DOWN THE
KINGDOM OF DARKNESS"

DR. JOSEPH R ROGERS SR.

MY ROLE
AS A
DEACON
THE DEACON'S ROLE: FROM
A BIBLICAL PERSPECTIVE
DR. JOSEPH R. ROGERS, SR.

Church Discipline
Guidelines
Dealing With Internal
Church Discipline
Holiness
Dr. Joseph R.
Rogers Sr.

DIVORCE
GOD'S WAY
(FROM A
BIBLICAL
PERSPECTIVE)

BLACK
HISTORY
MONTH
A Sermon Series S:
Black History/King Day
A Sermon Series Referencing
Black History Month/Martin
Luther King, Jr. Celebration

RENEWING YOUR
MIND: SPIRITUAL
INVENTORY
DR. JOSEPH R. ROGERS, SR.

MEN'S DAY
SERMON
OUTLINES S
SERMON OUTLINES
FOR EASY PREACHING
A few
good men
DR. JOSEPH R.
ROGERS, SR.

The Book Of
Revelations
Study Guide
THE UNVEILING OF
THE PROPHECY
DR. JOSEPH ROGERS, SR.

Insights For The Senior's Ministry
Understanding The Myths & Truths Of The Aging Process
Dr. Joseph R. Rogers Sr.

BLESSED AND HIGHLY FAVORED A STUDY SERIES: PHYSICAL & SPIRITUAL BLESSINGS
Dr. Joseph Rogers, Sr.

A Study Of The
Book Of Psalms
Study Series L
Understanding The
Hymns Of The Bible
The
Psalms
What To Do
With Our
Fears Tears
Guilt
Depression
Desires Joy
Dr. Joseph Roosevelt
Rogers, Sr.

"Whoso fineth a wife fineth
a good thing and obtaineth
favor of the Lord". (Proverbs
18:22)
Together
Forever
Insights For
Choosing A
Companion
Securing The
Right Companion
Dr. Joseph Roosevelt Rogers Sr.

VIII. Notes

Notes Con't.

www.ingramcontent.com/pod-product-compliance
Ingram Content Group UK Ltd.
Pitfield, Milton Keynes, MK11 3LW, UK
UKHW041924190726
13854UKWH00003B/1425

9 780359 000043